D0918356

Explore
Earth's
five oceans

Explore the Continents

Bobbie Kalman

🜎 Crabtree Publishing Company

www.crabtreebooks.com

A Bobbie Kalman Book

In memory of Karuna Thal, who shared my love of oceans.
You are always in my thoughts, beautiful Dolphin Girl!

Author and Editor-in-Chief
Bobbie Kalman

Editor
Kathy Middleton

Fact editor
Marcella Haanstra

Proofreader
Crystal Sikkens

Photo research
Bobbie Kalman

Design
Bobbie Kalman
Katherine Berti

Print and production coordinator
Katherine Berti

Prepress technician
Katherine Berti

Illustrations
Barbara Bedell: pages 9 (magnifying glass), 10–11 (blue fish, seahorse, butterflyfish, corals, lower humpback whale), 16 (humpback whale), 20, 26 (blue fish and seahorse)
Katherine Berti: pages 4, 10–11 (tern and seal), 16 (seal), 20, 26 (crab and map)
Robert MacGregor: pages 6, 16 (map)
Cori Marvin: page 20
Jeannette McNaughton-Julich: page 26 (dolphins)
Vanessa Parson-Robbs: page 20
Bonna Rouse: pages 10–11 (hatchet fish, anglerfish, vampirefish, seagull, sea turtle, lantern fish, squid, shrimp), 20, 26 (sea stars)
Margaret Amy Salter: pages 9 (phytoplankton), 10–11 (background and octopus), 20, 26 (yellow fish)
Tiffany Wybouw: pages 10–11 (orca, upper humpback whale), 26 (sea turtle)

Photographs
BigstockPhoto: page 15 (bottom)
Dreamstime: page 19 (top)
iStockphoto: pages 21 (top), 26 (shells except right)
NASA/Goddard Space Flight Center Scientific Visualization Studio: page 7
Photos.com: page 25 (bottom)
US Coast Guard: page 31
Cover and other images by Shutterstock

Library and Archives Canada Cataloguing in Publication

Kalman, Bobbie, 1947-
     Explore earth's five oceans / Bobbie Kalman.

(Explore the continents)
Includes index.
Issued also in an electronic format.
ISBN 978-0-7787-3077-4 (bound).--ISBN 978-0-7787-3091-0 (pbk.)

     1. Ocean--Juvenile literature. 2. Oceanography--Juvenile
literature. I. Title. II. Series: Explore the continents

GC21.5.K353 2011   j551.46   C2010-904118-6

Library of Congress Cataloging-in-Publication Data

Kalman, Bobbie.
   Explore earth's five oceans / Bobbie Kalman.
       p. cm. -- (Explore the continents)
   Includes index.
   ISBN 978-0-7787-3091-0 (pbk. : alk. paper) --
ISBN 978-0-7787-3077-4 (reinforced library binding : alk. paper)
-- ISBN 978-1-4271-9482-4 (electronic (pdf))
   1. Ocean--Juvenile literature. 2. Oceanography--Juvenile
literature. I. Title. II. Series.

   GC21.5.K3519 2010
   551.46--dc22
                                        2010024602

Crabtree Publishing Company

www.crabtreebooks.com   1-800-387-7650

Printed in the U.S.A./082010/BA20100709

Published in Canada
Crabtree Publishing
616 Welland Ave.
St. Catharines, Ontario
L2M 5V6

Published in the United States
Crabtree Publishing
PMB 59051
350 Fifth Avenue, 59th Floor
New York, New York 10118

Published in the United Kingdom
Crabtree Publishing
Maritime House
Basin Road North, Hove
BN41 1WR

Published in Australia
Crabtree Publishing
386 Mt. Alexander Rd.
Ascot Vale (Melbourne)
VIC 3032

Contents

Five oceans on Earth

Earth is called the "blue planet" because it looks blue from space. It looks blue because water covers about three-quarters of Earth. The blue areas on the map below show where water is on Earth. The largest areas of water are called **oceans**.

*Oceans flow around seven huge areas of land. These areas are called **continents**. The continents are Africa, Europe, Asia, South America, North America, Antarctica, and Australia/Oceania. Find the continents on the map below.*

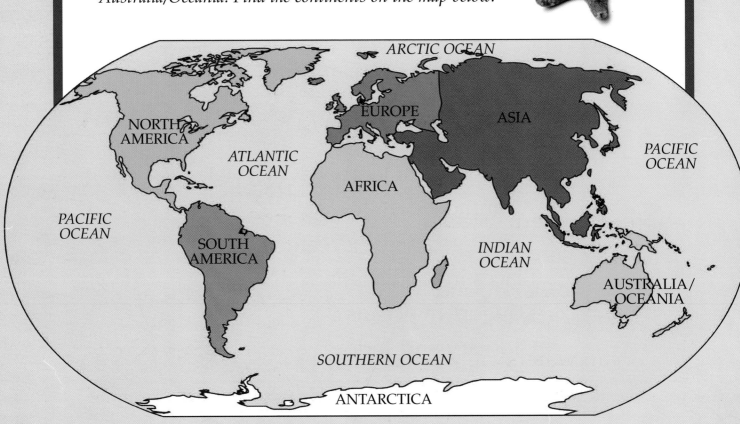

ARCTIC OCEAN

NORTH AMERICA

EUROPE

ASIA

ATLANTIC OCEAN

PACIFIC OCEAN

AFRICA

PACIFIC OCEAN

SOUTH AMERICA

INDIAN OCEAN

AUSTRALIA/ OCEANIA

SOUTHERN OCEAN

ANTARCTICA

These children are swimming in an ocean. They are playing in the ocean waves.

Five oceans

There are five oceans on Earth. From smallest to largest, they are the Arctic Ocean, the Southern Ocean, the Indian Ocean, the Atlantic Ocean, and the Pacific Ocean. Some ocean waters are warm. Others are covered with ice.

These fur seals live in the Southern Ocean. Most of this ocean is covered with ice for at least six months of the year.

Directions on Earth

There are four main **directions** on Earth. The four main directions are north, south, east, and west. The most northern place on Earth is the **North Pole**. The most southern place on Earth is the **South Pole**. In areas near the North Pole and the South Pole, ocean waters are cold or frozen.

N

W ← → E

S

NORTH POLE

NORTHERN HEMISPHERE

EQUATOR

SOUTHERN HEMISPHERE

Hot near the equator

Areas near the **equator** are always hot. The equator is an imaginary line that separates Earth into two equal parts. The oceans near the equator are very warm.

SOUTH POLE

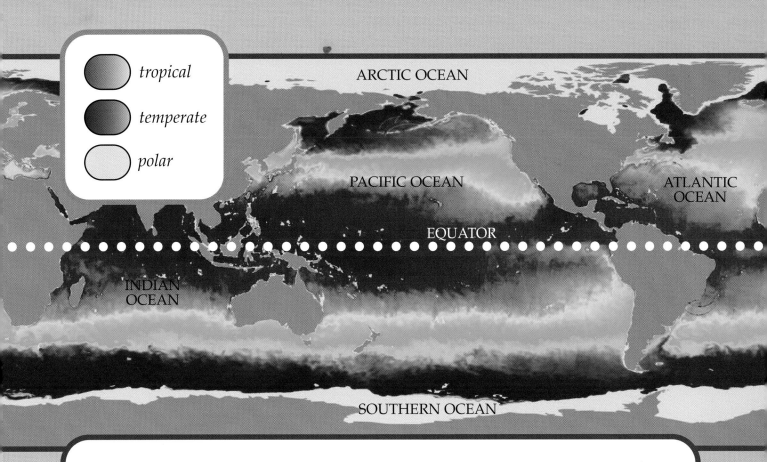

The colored parts of this map show the world's oceans. The red waters are **tropical**. They are the warmest because they are near the equator. The white areas are **polar**, or near the poles. These oceans are cold and icy. The **temperate** ocean waters are in areas with four seasons. These ocean areas are warm in summer and cold in winter.

The northern part

The part of Earth that is between the equator and the North Pole is called the **Northern Hemisphere**. The Arctic Ocean and parts of the Atlantic Ocean and Pacific Ocean are in the Northern Hemisphere.

The southern part

The **Southern Hemisphere** is the part of Earth that is between the equator and the South Pole. The Indian Ocean, Southern Ocean, and parts of the Atlantic Ocean and Pacific Ocean are in the Southern Hemisphere.

One big ocean!

The five oceans make up one big "world ocean" because they are all connected to one another. The waters are always moving. As wind blows across the top of oceans, it pushes the water. The water moves in waves. As the water moves, it helps heat the air and land in winter and cool the air and land in summer.

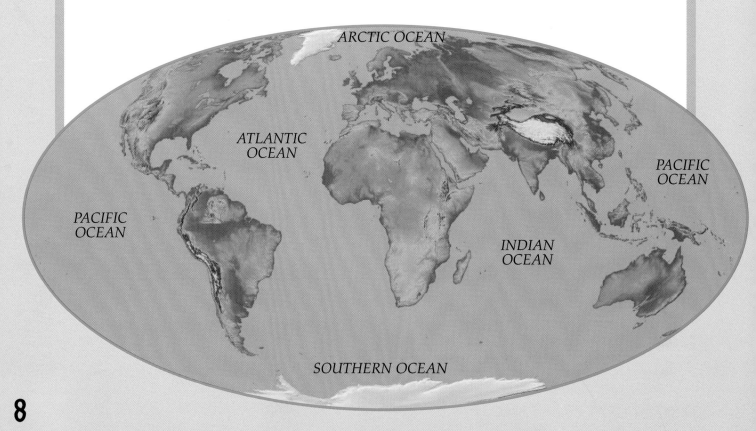

ARCTIC OCEAN

ATLANTIC
OCEAN

PACIFIC
OCEAN

PACIFIC
OCEAN

INDIAN
OCEAN

SOUTHERN OCEAN

What are seas?

Seas are parts of oceans that are close to land. The South China Sea, the Caribbean Sea, and the Mediterranean Sea are three very large seas. The water in both oceans and seas is **salt water**. Salt water has a lot of salt in it.

This picture shows part of the Mediterranean Sea along the coast of Italy.

Making oxygen

Half of the world's supply of **oxygen** is made in oceans. Oxygen is the part of air that animals and people need to breathe. The oxygen in oceans is made by **phytoplankton**, which are tiny plants too small to see with just our eyes. Many kinds of ocean animals eat these tiny plants.

phytoplankton

Zones in oceans

Some parts of oceans are very deep, and some are shallow. The parts of oceans that are shallow receive a lot of sunlight. Sunlight travels down through the water, but it cannot reach the deeper **zones**, or sections.

Life in the zones

Plants need light to make food. They can survive only in the **sunlit zone**, the top zone of the ocean. Most of the animals that live in oceans live in this top zone. Very little sunlight reaches the **twilight zone**. The water here is cold, as well as dark. In the **midnight zone**, the water is very dark and almost freezing cold. These pages show some of the animals that live in the different ocean zones.

tern

dolphin

seal

sunlit zone

twilight zone

midnight zone

hatchet fish

anglerfish

vampirefish

Learn more about animals that live
in the sunlit zone on pages 20-21.

seagull

whale

seahorse

orca

sea turtle

coral

butterflyfish

lantern fish

Some large whales,
such as humpbacks,
can dive deep into
the midnight zone.

bioluminescent
squid

bioluminescent
sea jelly

Very few animals can live in the cold, dark
waters of the midnight zone. Octopuses, sea
jellies, and squids are some animals that live in
the deep parts of oceans. Some of these animals
can make their own light. The giving off of light
by a living thing is called **bioluminescence**.
Some sea jellies and squids are bioluminescent.

deep sea
shrimp

11

The Arctic Ocean

The Arctic Ocean is the smallest and shallowest of the five oceans. It surrounds the North Pole and touches the continents of Europe, Asia, and North America. Parts of the United States (Alaska), Canada, Russia, Iceland, Norway, and Greenland touch the Arctic Ocean.

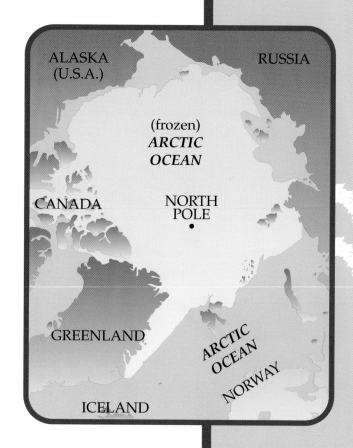

ALASKA (U.S.A.)

RUSSIA

(frozen) *ARCTIC OCEAN*

CANADA

NORTH POLE

GREENLAND

ARCTIC OCEAN

NORWAY

ICELAND

*The temperatures at the North Pole are so cold that the top of the ocean freezes into floating chunks of sea ice called **ice floes**. This harp seal mother and baby are on **pack ice**. Pack ice is thick ice that forms when ice floes freeze together.*

Icebergs

This polar bear is sitting on top of an **iceberg**. An iceberg is a piece of ice that has broken off a **glacier** and is floating in water. A glacier is a slow-moving river of ice that has formed on land.

Arctic Ocean animals

Many kinds of fish and other animals live under the ice in the Arctic Ocean. Octopuses, squid, and sea jellies are just some of these. Whales also live in the icy waters. They have a thick layer of **blubber**, or fat, under their skin to keep them warm. Some whales leave the Arctic Ocean in winter, but narwhals and beluga whales stay, unless the ocean freezes over completely.

beluga whale

A narwhal is a toothed whale that has a long tusk growing out of the left side of its upper jaw. Male narwhals have tusks. Only a few female narwhals have them.

male narwhal

female narwhal with calf

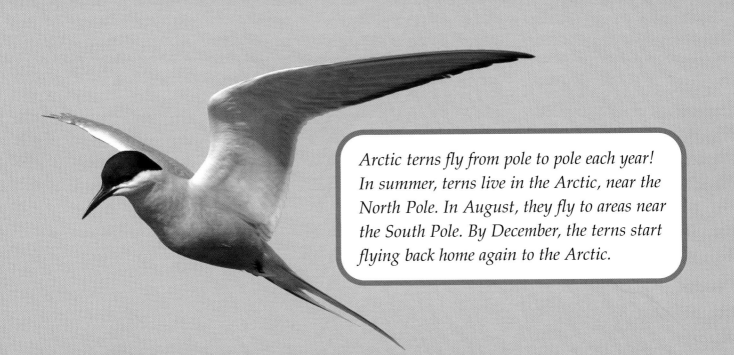

Arctic terns fly from pole to pole each year! In summer, terns live in the Arctic, near the North Pole. In August, they fly to areas near the South Pole. By December, the terns start flying back home again to the Arctic.

Polar bears are well suited to swimming in polar oceans. Their fur is oily and waterproof. Just like whales, polar bears have a thick layer of blubber to keep them warm.

The Southern Ocean

The cold Southern Ocean surrounds the South Pole and the continent of Antarctica. It is the second-smallest of the five oceans and is at the opposite end of the Earth from the Arctic Ocean. There are seas around Antarctica. See the seas on the map below.

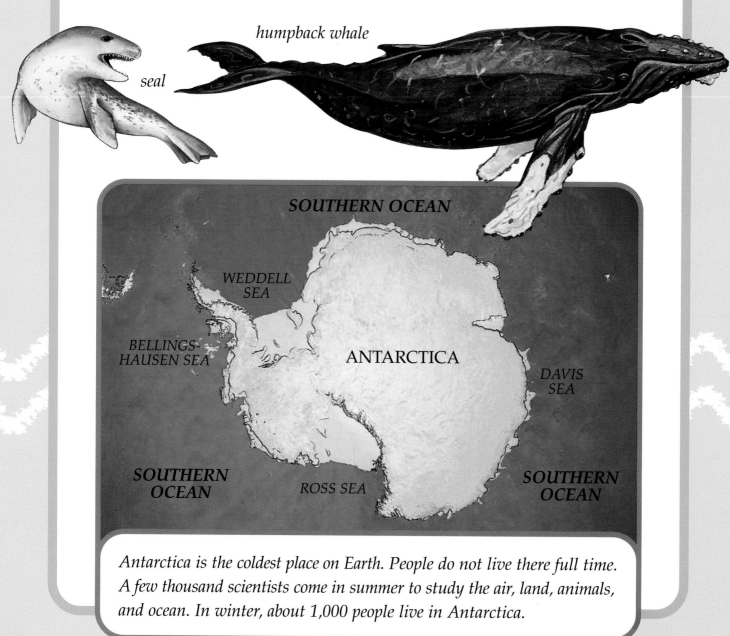

seal

humpback whale

SOUTHERN OCEAN

WEDDELL SEA

BELLINGS-HAUSEN SEA

ANTARCTICA

DAVIS SEA

SOUTHERN OCEAN

ROSS SEA

SOUTHERN OCEAN

Antarctica is the coldest place on Earth. People do not live there full time. A few thousand scientists come in summer to study the air, land, animals, and ocean. In winter, about 1,000 people live in Antarctica.

Plenty of penguins

The Arctic Ocean and Southern Ocean are not very different from one another. Both are covered with ice for most of the year. Seals, whales, and some sea birds live in both oceans. Penguins live in the Southern Ocean, but they do not live in the Arctic Ocean. Polar bears live in the Arctic Ocean, but not in the Southern Ocean.

Emperor penguins live in the Southern Ocean. They travel onto land to have their babies. Both parents care for the baby birds.

*This **colony**, or large group, of emperor penguins has gathered on sea ice in the Weddell Sea in Antarctica.*

The Indian Ocean

The Indian Ocean is the third-biggest of Earth's five oceans. It is also the warmest. The Indian Ocean touches the continents of Australia/Oceania, Africa, and Asia. The Atlantic Ocean, Pacific Ocean, and Southern Ocean flow into the Indian Ocean.

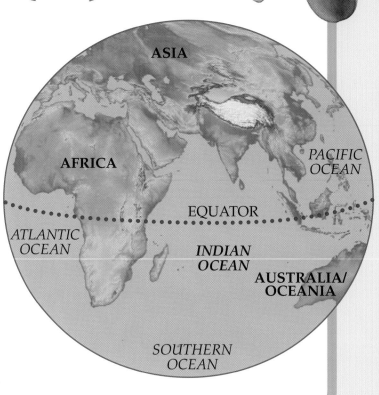

The water near the shores of tropical oceans is shallow and clear.

*The city of Durban, South Africa, is on the Indian Ocean. The ocean there is warm and contains beautiful **coral reefs** (see pages 20-21).*

INDIAN OCEAN

INDONESIAN ARCHIPELAGO

Thousands of islands

There are thousands of islands in the Indian Ocean. The country of Indonesia, for example, is made up of 17,508 islands! The Indonesian **Archipelago** lies between the Indian Ocean and the Pacific Ocean. An archipelago is a chain of islands in a body of water, such as an ocean.

Coral reefs

The Indian Ocean has many islands and coral reefs. Most coral reefs grow close to islands that were created by **volcanoes** (see page 27). Coral reefs are huge underwater structures found in warm tropical waters. They are **habitats** with many kinds of fish and other animals. A habitat is a natural place where animals live. Corals look like rocks or colorful plants, but they are made up of tiny animals called coral **polyps**.

island

coral reef

Many kinds of colorful fish live in coral reefs in the Indian Ocean.

This hawksbill sea turtle is feeding on sponges in a coral reef.

The Atlantic Ocean

The Atlantic Ocean is the second-biggest ocean on Earth. It lies between the Arctic Ocean and Southern Ocean and touches the continents of North America, South America, Europe, and Africa. Parts of the Atlantic Ocean are tropical, parts are temperate, and the northern and southern parts are polar.

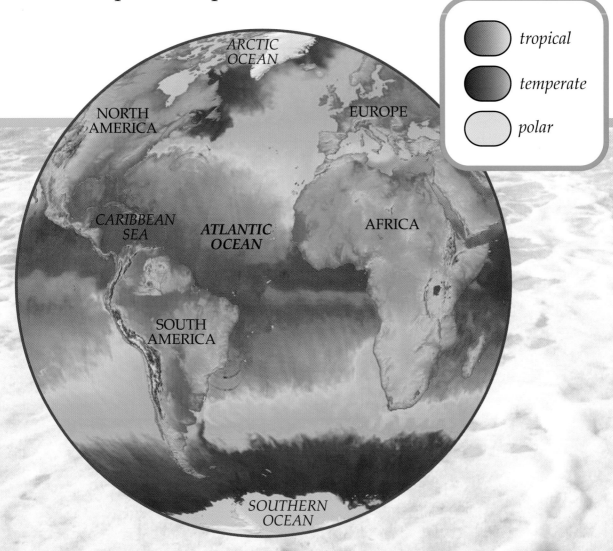

tropical

temperate

polar

ARCTIC OCEAN

NORTH AMERICA

EUROPE

CARIBBEAN SEA

ATLANTIC OCEAN

AFRICA

SOUTH AMERICA

SOUTHERN OCEAN

The Caribbean Sea is part of the Atlantic Ocean. It is a tropical sea, which touches North and South America. The waters are warm all year.

In winter, the parts of the Atlantic Ocean that are near the poles are cold. This iceberg is in the Atlantic Ocean near Newfoundland, Canada.

23

Atlantic waters

The water in oceans is always moving. **Currents** are like rivers of water that flow through oceans. Warm currents that flow from tropical oceans warm up the temperate and polar oceans. Cold currents that flow from cold oceans cool down the water in tropical areas. The Gulf Stream is a fast Atlantic Ocean current that brings warm water from Florida up the east coast of North America. It then crosses the Atlantic Ocean, warming the **climate** of western Europe.

Hurricanes form in the warm Atlantic Ocean. They are huge storms with strong, spinning winds. They often blow over land and destroy towns and cities. Hurricane Katrina, in 2005, was one of the worst hurricanes ever in the United States. It destroyed much of New Orleans, as well as other cities in Louisiana, Mississippi, and Alabama.

Viking ship

Between old and new

Today, most people travel from Europe to North America or South America by airplane. In the past, people sailed across the Atlantic Ocean from the Old World (Europe) to the New World (the Americas). The first **explorers**, the Vikings, sailed to North America around the year 1,000. In 1492, Christopher Columbus crossed the Atlantic from Europe to the Bahamas. Since then, many people from Europe have sailed to North and South America. Some came to visit, and others came to start new lives. It took them weeks to cross the rough Atlantic Ocean to their new homes in the Americas.

Christopher Columbus's ship

This boy is waving goodbye to his family in Europe. He is being taken by rowboat to a ship in which he will cross the ocean.

The huge Pacific Ocean!

The Pacific Ocean is the biggest ocean on Earth. It takes up about one-third of the Earth's surface and is larger than all the land on Earth put together. The Pacific Ocean stretches from the Arctic Ocean to the Southern Ocean. It contains between 20,000 to 30,000 islands. Most are around the equator.

The Pacific Ocean touches the continents of Asia, North America, South America, and Australia/Oceania.

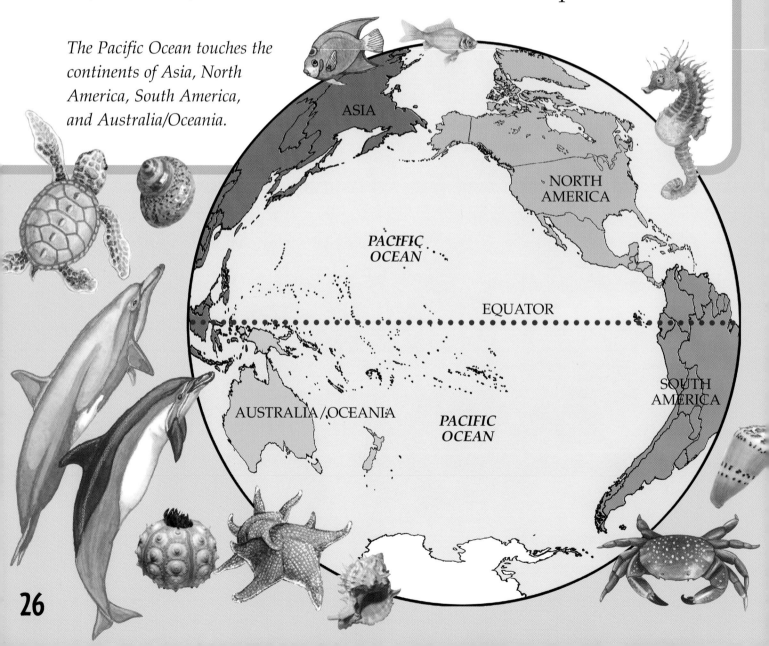

ASIA

NORTH AMERICA

PACIFIC OCEAN

EQUATOR

SOUTH AMERICA

AUSTRALIA/OCEANIA

PACIFIC OCEAN

The Pacific Ring of Fire

More than half of Earth's **active** volcanoes are in the Pacific Ocean. A volcano is an opening in Earth's **crust**, or outer layer. Hot **magma**, ash, and gases escape out of a volcano. The Pacific Ring of Fire has 452 volcanoes. Parts of Asia, North America, South America, and Australia/Oceania are in the Ring of Fire. The map below shows this area.

magma

An active volcano is one that has erupted not long ago, is erupting often, or could erupt at any time.

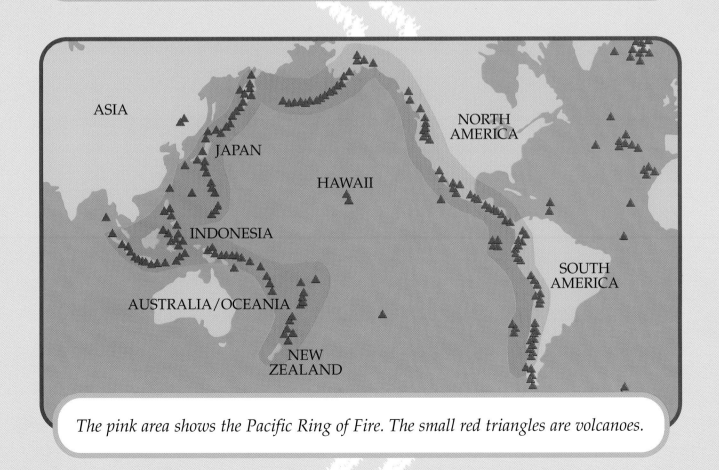

The pink area shows the Pacific Ring of Fire. The small red triangles are volcanoes.

Places in the Pacific

The **Pacific Rim** is made up of countries and cities that are located around the edge of the Pacific Ocean. How many of these places do you know?

*The Hawaiian Islands are actually the top parts of underwater volcanoes. After many eruptions, the volcanoes rose above the water to form islands. Diamond Head is on the island of Oahu. It is the **crater** of a volcano.*

The city of Vancouver is in British Columbia, Canada. British Columbia is a province on the coast of the Pacific Ocean.

Australia's biggest city, Sydney, is on the Tasman Sea, which is part of the South Pacific Ocean.

marine iguanas

The Galapagos Islands are at the equator in the eastern Pacific Ocean. The islands formed from volcanoes. The Galapagos are known for the many kinds of animals that live there, such as these marine iguanas and the dancing blue-footed booby.

blue-footed booby

Hong Kong is in China. It is on the South China Sea, which is a part of the Pacific Ocean.

Dangers in oceans

Oceans can be dangerous places! Hurricanes form over oceans and can destroy towns and cities. **Tsunamis** can be even more destructive. Tsunamis are caused by **volcanic eruptions** or **earthquakes** in the ocean. When either of these events takes place, the water in the ocean forms waves. The waves become huge walls of water by the time they reach land. These powerful waves knock down everything in their path and flood the land with water.

In 2004, a huge earthquake under the Indian Ocean caused the "Asian Tsunami Disaster." The tsunami killed more than 230,000 people in fourteen countries and destroyed hundreds of thousands of homes. Indonesia was the hardest hit.

Hurricane and oil spill

In 2005, Hurricane Katrina caused massive damage in Louisiana, Mississippi, and Alabama. In April 2010, an explosion in an oil rig under the ocean caused hundreds of millions of gallons of oil to leak into the Gulf of Mexico, which is part of the Atlantic Ocean. The oil has killed animals in the ocean and on shore and covered the beaches of the Gulf with thick oil. Many people have lost their businesses and jobs because they cannot fish any longer. Some people became ill from breathing the **fumes**, or gases, given off by the oil. This disaster shows us why we need to stop using oil and start using clean sources of energy now!

Glossary

Note: Some boldfaced words are defined in the book.

archipelago A chain of islands

bioluminescence The glow of light made inside some animals such as sea jellies

blubber A thick layer of fat under an animal's skin

climate The long-time usual weather in an area

crater The large opening at the top of a volcano

crust The outer layer of hard rock that covers Earth

earthquake The violent shaking of the ground that can destroy buildings

explorer A person who traveled the world looking for new lands to discover

magma Hot liquid rock deep inside Earth

polar Describing waters with cold temperatures near the poles

temperate Describing waters with changing temperatures during the four seasons

tropical Describing very warm waters near the equator

tsunami Huge ocean waves that cause flooding on land

volcanic eruption The release of magma, gases, ash, and rocks from a volcano

Index

Learn more about Earth's oceans from these other books in the **Explore the Continents** series.